How to Change the Name of a Minor in Texas

By Attorney Richard S. Granat

FIRST EDITION   SEPTEMBER 2014

Editor   Pamela Andrews

Technology   Gregor Weeks

Cover Design   GRANATDESIGN, LLC.

Printing   Amazon Services

SmartLegalForms is an imprint of SmartLegalForms®, Inc.
SmartLegalForms is a trademark of SmartLegalForms®, Inc.
Manufactured in the United States of America

Granat, Richard

How to Change the Name of a Minor in Texas / by Richard S. Granat -1st ed.

Registration Code: 20142054

UPDATE SERVICE AND FILLABLE FORMS

All legal content in this product was up-to-date during publication. If you register your product using the Registration Code on this page and your email address at http://www.texasnamechangelaw.com you will receive any legal form updates since this book was published and you can download the legal forms in Adobe .PDF fillable format for no additional charge. This is a free service.

If you purchase this book online and we have your email address your product is registered automatically and you will be sent a free copy of the Adobe .PDF fillable forms automatically. We don't use your email address for any other purpose other than to communicate with you about these legal forms.

Please note this self-help legal formbook is not a substitute for personalized legal advice from a lawyer who practices in the jurisdiction where you live. We do not provide legal advice.

Table of Contents

Introduction to Name Change for a Minor in Texas

n Texas, a parent, managing conservator, or guardian who wishes to change the name of a minor child must file a Petition in the District Court of the county where the minor child resides. A Petition informs the Court of the Petitioner's name, the name to be assumed, the reasons for the change and other personal information required by statute. The Petition must be notarized.

Adults petitioning on behalf of the minor should include one or both parents, or managing conservators, guardians or other persons given legal rights to the child in a court order. These forms are for uncontested name change actions. All Petitioners must agree to the name change and join and sign the petition in the presence of a Notary.

IMPORTANT NOTE: If the parents of the children are single, separated or divorced, both parents still must consent and join the petition for the name change action. A parent who has "sole custody" of the minor child still must petition with the other parent. Exceptions to one or both parents joining the petition would be if one or both parents had their rights to the children terminated by court order or if the parents are deceased. (Note: a copy of such court order or a death certificate will likely need to be provided to the Court in these instances.)

These documents, and accompanying explanations and filing instructions have been compiled for Petitioners seeking a name change for a minor child. Petitioners may 1) use these documents and represent themselves "pro se" (that is, without the assistance of an attorney); 2) use these documents and seek legal review and advice from a licensed attorney in the state; or 3) use these documents and obtain legal counsel to assist with the legal action.

The law which governs name changes in Texas is Texas Family Code, chapter 45. The Courts are often willing to accept name changes for almost any legitimate reason. However, granting a Petition for Change of Name is discretionary with the Court. For an order of name change to be granted, the Court must find compliance with the requirements of notice and the requirements for the allegations in the Petition. The Court must also find good and sufficient reason for the change and find the change consistent with the public interest.

Once you file your Petition for Name Change of a Minor, schedule a time to ask the Judge to approve the name change. The Court conducts a hearing and then renders final judgment by entering an Order of approval of name change.

County Variations

Except where specifically noted, we have attempted to include every document that you will need to file for the name change. These documents and instructions have been designed to meet the requirements set by Texas. It is possible that county variations exist in the documents and/or filing instructions. Some variation in terminology may also exist (some counties may use a Petition, while others may use a Complaint, even though they are the same document). We are not able to plan for every possible county variation. Please understand that adjustments may need to be made to meet variations to local documents and/or procedures. Please work with your court clerk to ensure that adjustments are accurate.

Eligibility for Changing Your Child's Name in Texas

Requirements to File for a Change of Name for a Minor in Texas

Texas law requires certain things before you can file for a name change (for a minor) and/or during the name change process in Texas. These requirements include:

- Name change actions for a minor are filed in the District Court within the county where the minor resides. There is no residency timeframe which must be met to change the child's name.

- The minor must not have been convicted of any crime, felony and/or misdemeanor.

- The minor must not be under indictment for a crime, felony and/or misdemeanor.

- You must not be requesting the name change (for a minor) to avoid creditors.

- The minor must not be involved in a bankruptcy proceeding.

- The child must be a minor, 17 years of age or younger.

- If the child is age 10 or older, he or she must sign a Consent to the name change.

Exceptions for this Product

If you are only correcting a first or middle name AND you were born in Texas, you may NOT need to go through the court-ordered process. We recommend that you contact the Vital Records Department/Agency in Texas. Contact information for the Texas State Vital Records Office can be found at http://www.vitalrec.com/tx.html. You may also want to contact your local Court Clerk for further information.

Adoptions, Paternity Actions, and Minor Name Changes

If the minor child's name is being changed as part of an adoption proceeding, these forms will not be needed. The minor's name would be changed as part of the Adoption Order. Similarly, a child's name would be changed as part of a paternity action if so ordered by the Court.

Frequently Asked Questions about Name Change

Changing Your Child's Name

A parent, guardian, or managing conservator may change the name of a minor if the change is not for a fraudulent purpose. Reasons for a name change are varied and personal, but it must be in the best interest of the child. The child may dislike his given name, want his name to reflect his heritage or religious views, want to name to be the same of a step-parent, or may need to change it for security and protection purposes.

Laws require courts to grant an application for a name change unless a prohibition does not allow the change. For instance, a minor convicted of a felony cannot change his name since law enforcement has a substantial interest in tracking his location.

Most states require a court order to legalize a name change, so contact your local Clerk of Court to find out whether your particular state allows name change by common usage.

TIP

Remember although your state might allow name change by common usage, obtaining a court order may save a lot of trouble in the long run. The new name will be easier to prove and is more likely to be accepted if you have a court order to back it up. Your bank may be reluctant to change your child's name on your bank account if you have no court order evidencing the name change.

Can I pick any name for my minor child?

Yes, but there are a few limitations:
- The name cannot be chosen with fraudulent intent. Any type of judgments against the minor will not be avoided by changing the name.
- The name cannot be intentionally confusing, such as one with numbers or symbols. This means no person cannot refer to himself as "&" (ampersand); however, the symbol will never be his legal name, e.g., it will not ever appear on a passport.
- The name cannot be a racial slur, nor can it contain threatening or obscure words, or words likely to incite violence. Names that are obscene or vulgar cannot be

legally obtained. A person may use such a name, but he cannot have his name legally changed.

- The name cannot interfere with any trademarked name or with the rights of another (i.e. such as the rights of a celebrity).

What are the fees involved with a name change application?

Charges you may incur in filing any legal pleading with a court could include: filing fees, postage for certified mailings, fees associated with the signatures and seals of a Notary Public, publication fees and service of process charges. It is difficult to determine exactly what fees will be needed due to the varying circumstances surrounding any legal action or case. The processes and requirements for a name change application vary sometimes from county to county or even courthouse to courthouse. We recommend that you contact your local Court Clerk for information regarding the exact current cost of these fees.

How long will the entire application for change of name take?

Name change actions can take a day to six months (sometimes even longer). The time it takes for such action to be ordered/decreed varies not only from county to county, but sometimes from courthouse to courthouse. Should time be a major factor for you, to see how long a name change at your local courthouse will take to process, we recommend that you contact the courthouse where you anticipate filing your particular legal action.

Can the entire procedure take place online or will a court appearance be necessary?

You should file the name change forms in-person at the local courthouse where the minor child resides. This is the fastest, easiest and best approach to filing. Besides appearing to file your documents/forms, name change actions often require other appearances within court. In Texas, a hearing is usually held for a minor's name to be changed.

If you have further questions regarding court appearances pertaining to a name change application, we recommend that you contact your local Court Clerk with your questions.

If the child was born in Florida but has since moved to Texas, in which state should I file the application for change of name?

To file for a name change, one must meet the residency requirements of the state in which he/she wishes to file. In order to petition a state for name change, you must typically be a permanent resident of that state. To file for a minor's name to be changed in Texas, the documents must be filed in the county where the minor child resides (in Texas). Proof of the child's residency may be required from the Court.

I am only interested in changing my child's first name. Do your forms apply to this circumstance?

Our name change forms can be used for changes of the first name, middle name, last name and/or any combination. The correcting of a first or middle name on a birth certificate may have a simpler procedure (see the "Exceptions" section for more information).

Are your name change forms appropriate in adoption proceedings or paternity actions?

Our name change products and services are not intended for an adoption or paternity action, since in such cases the name change should be done as part of the proceeding.

What if someone files an objection to my request?

If anyone files an objection to your request, the case will become a contested case and you are strongly urged to hire an attorney. If you retain no attorney you will have to represent yourself in a contested hearing.

What if the request to change my child's name is denied?

Most name change Petitions are granted, however, the law gives the Court the power to decline a person's request for a name change. Therefore, the Court can refuse a name change request if there is a reason to decline the request.

If a name change Petition was denied because there was not enough evidence to support the request, then you will have to wait until the circumstances that led to the denial change before you can file another Petition. This is because once the Court decides about an incident or an event; it cannot address that same incident or event again. If the Petition was denied because of a procedural error (you did not file the correct forms), then you should correct the error and request another time to ask the Judge to approve your child's name change.

Finally, whenever you lose in court, you may request the Court to reconsider its decision and you may appeal the decision to a higher Court. In most cases you have 30 days or less from the Judge's decision to exercise these rights or you may lose your right to reconsideration or appeal. Seek the assistance of an attorney to exercise these rights.

What do I have to do after my child receives the new name?

The first step for a minor is to obtain a new Social Security card with the minor's new name. This will help to facilitate changing the minor's name with other agencies, schools, and institutions. You can start by applying at your local Social Security office. You will need to bring proof of the minor's former name and the court order authorizing the change in name. To obtain a new driver's license, you must present a certified copy of the Court Order to the Department of Motor Vehicle office in Texas.

Then, you need to contact any government agencies with which you or your child deals to notify them of the child's new name and request it be changed in their records. Some important agencies to notify are doctor's offices, the child's school, any creditors, banks and financial institutions, insurance companies, post office, etc.

You may also need to notify the passport office and Bureau of Records or Vital Statistics (to obtain a birth certificate with the new name). Change the name on any legal papers, such as wills, trusts, or contracts. More information on this topic may is offered in a separate section.

TIP

Although some agencies will change a name in their records with just a phone call, most will require a written request indicating the new name and a copy of the court judgment legalizing it. To save yourself time, prepare a form letter clearly stating your child's old name and new name, and request that you want the child to be known by his or her new name. Also, make several copies of the judgment authorizing the name change so that you can readily provide it to any agency or business that requests proof of the legal name change.

Can I obtain a birth certificate with my child's new name?

Yes. However, the laws in your state may only permit issuance of an amended birth certificate rather than a new original birth certificate.

Is it possible to have a new passport issued reflecting my child's name change?

Yes. You must apply for an amended passport for your child by completing a Passport Amendment/Validation Application (Form DS-19). Provide a certified copy of the court order and your child's existing passport.

I changed my child's name last year but do not like it as much as I thought I would. Can I change it back?

Probably, but follow the same procedure required for you to have changed it. Remember that discretion to allow a name change rests with the Court, and the Court will not look favorably on frequent name changes. Select a name you and/or your child likes and will be comfortable using.

Forms and Detailed Filing Instructions

Getting Started

All of your documents will eventually be filed in the District Court in the jurisdiction in which the minor child resides. Proof of the child's residency may be requested from the Court.

Here is some information obtain from the Clerk's office prior to filing your documents:

1. Obtain the mailing address of the Court and the street address if it differs from the mailing address. Also, obtain driving directions if need be.

2. Ask the cost of the required filing fee. The fee sometimes differs from county to county.

3. Ask if you need to file documents specific to your local Court with the standard Texas documents we have included. If there are additional documents, find out how you can obtain them.

4. Ask if there are any other special filing requirements you should know of. Some counties, such as Travis County and Montgomery County, require that all civil cases filed in the District Court Clerk's office shall have attached a Civil Case Information Sheet prepared by the District Court Clerk. Additionally, they require that all pleadings, motions, orders and other papers, including exhibits attached thereto, when offered for filing or entry, shall be descriptively titled and punched at the top of the page to accommodate Clerk's 2.75" center-to-center flat-filing system. By calling your local District Court in advance, you will know of such requirements upon filing.

5. Ask how many copies of each document or form are required. The majority of Courts only require the original – some may require an additional copy or two. (NOTE: Even if only the original is required, it is always a good idea to have extra copies on-hand.)

The Forms

This book contains all of the forms you need to change the name of a minor in Texas.

The form set includes the following forms:

Texas Civil Case Information Sheet -- The included Civil Case Information Sheet is only a sample document. The Civil Case Information Sheet usually varies from county to county. If your Court will not accept our general document, obtain your Court's local variation of the Civil Case Information Sheet upon your first filing and complete this document in black ink.

Child's Consent to Change Name -- If the minor is at least 10 years old, he or she must provide written consent to the Court. If the minor is younger, the petitioning adult can sue without the minor's written consent. This document should be completed, signed by the minor in the presence of a Notary, and filed as part of the initial filing.

Affidavit of Self-Representation -- This document may be required if you are representing yourself (pro se) for the minor's name change. This also may be needed if you received legal review and advice from an attorney (limited representation).

Agreed Order Changing a Name of a Minor – Once signed, this document makes the name change official. The Judge may sign this document, or the Court may provide their own. This is the final decree of name change.

Order Setting and Hearing Form -- A hearing may be required in minor name change actions. County and local procedures may vary. Some counties require that a hearing is officially scheduled by filing a related order. We have included a sample Order for this purpose. The Order used in your county may differ. The sample we have provided may need to be revised or replaced. Further details of Court hearings can be found later in the book (see **The Hearing, If Necessary**). You may also wish to discuss hearings, and the format and content of the Order document, with your local Court Clerk.

Affidavit of Publication

Your local jurisdiction may require a published notice of the child's proposed name change. This must be done to alert the public and give anyone who may contest the name change a chance to come forward. If this is required from your jurisdiction, your Court Clerk should be able to explain the requirements and provide access to any local documents not included in this state-specific questionnaire. If your Court Clerk cannot provide the publication documents, your local newspaper may be more helpful.

Completing the Forms

Since the forms are straightforward and self-explanatory, we have not provided line-by-line instructions for completing each item of the forms. However, we have included the following instructions to help you complete certain sections of the forms:

1. **Cause No.:** The Clerk of the Court will complete this section when you file your papers. Since you have no Cause Number yet these spaces should remain blank for now. However, if in the future you must file additional documents as part of this same name change action, insert the number(s) assigned by the Court.

2. **Judicial District:** Again, the Clerk of the Court will complete this section when you file your papers. Since you have no Judicial District yet these spaces should remain blank for now (as noted above, insert this number on any additional documents filed).

3. **Petitioner(s):** The name(s) of the Petitioner(s) will be indicated in the applicable sections. Where there are selections as to whether the Petitioner is a parent (a biological parent), a managing conservator (court-ordered conservator), or a legal guardian (court-ordered legal guardian), make the applicable selection with a check mark. Stepparents are not typically included in name change actions unless all legal rights to the minor child have been terminated by the biological parent(s), and the stepparent has legal (court-ordered) rights to the minor child. NOTE: All names listed in the documents (Petitioner, child current name and child requested name, etc.) should be the full names, including first, middle, and last.

4. **Street Address:** Enter the minor child's Texas street address and include any unit or apartment number if applicable. A physical address must be provided. A "P.O. Box" or other mailing address cannot be used. If the Petitioner(s) do not reside at the same residence as the minor child, that information will be entered as details for the Petitioner(s) in the applicable sections.

5. **County:** Enter the name of the minor child's county of residence. Do not add the word "County" after the name.

6. **Date, City, and State of Birth:** After the date of birth, enter the city and state where the minor child was born.

7. **Driver's License (if applicable):** Designate the license number and state of issue for each driver's license the minor child has possessed in the past 10 years (one entry at a time). Enter the current driver's license number first, then list any past licenses in chronological order from newest to oldest. Obviously if your minor child has no driver's license omit this field.

8. **Continuing Jurisdiction:** Under Chapter 155 of the Texas Family Code, the Court will have continuing jurisdiction if the child is the subject of a final order from a previous legal matter (such as divorce or custody). There are some exceptions such as dismissed cases involving the parent-child relationship. If applicable, enter the information in the fields provided, or if not applicable, make the selection that the child is not under continuing jurisdiction.

9. **Reason for Change of Name:** Remember that the Court will only grant the name change if it is in "the best interests of the child." Here are examples of acceptable reasons to change a child's name:

Example 1: We, the child's biological parents, have married since our child's birth and wish our child to share our family last name now.

Example 2: (Child's name) is mature enough to choose his/her own name and wishes to be known by his/her proposed name. Petitioner(s) consent(s) to this change of name and also prefer the proposed name.

Example 3: My son has always been known by his middle name, not his first name. I would like to reverse the names legally.

10. Texas Civil Case Information Sheet: The included Civil Case Information Sheet is only a sample document. The Civil Case Information Sheet usually varies from county to county. If your court will not accept our general document, obtain your court's local variation of the Civil Case Information Sheet upon your first filing and complete this document in black ink.

All date spaces for certifying, filing, etc., should be left blank. Such spaces have to be filled-in later (in black ink) when certifying (notarizing), filing, etc. The Clerk may even date-stamp your documents when you file. In light of such, we recommend that all dates like this be left blank - since they have to be filled-in on the date the document is filed, notarized, etc.

The Petition should NOT be signed outside of the presence of a Notary Public. Your signature must be witnessed and notarized by the Notary. Similarly, if the child is age 10 or over, the Child's Consent form must be completed and signed in the presence of a Notary. (Most courts and banks have a Notary Public on staff that can help you. The fee is usually not more than a few dollars or less per document.) NOTE: Make no copies of the documents until the documents are notarized. Upon signing the Petition, in front of the Notary, your Petition now becomes a Verified Petition.

Important Note! Get your documents notarized. Failure to do so is the most common reason for being denied a change of name.

Make copies of each of the documents. You will keep the copies for your records and bring them to court with you upon each appearance or filing. It is recommended to make at least three copies of each of these documents. Again, do not make copies of documents until they are notarized.

Overview of the Filing Process

1. Complete and print the documents. There are two sets of forms. The first set of forms is designed for joint petitioners. The second set of forms is to be used by a sole petitioner. NOTE: A copy of the child's birth certificate must be provided to the Court.

2. All Petitioners must sign documents in the presence of a Notary Public. If a Minor's Consent to Change Name is applicable (if the minor is at least 10 years old), this document must also be signed in the presence of a Notary Public.

3. Contact your local Court Clerk to learn more about the process, number of copies, filing fee, etc.

4. Take the documents to your local District Court for filing.

5. File the documents and pay the filing fee.

6. If required, arrange to have a notice published for several weeks, announcing the proposed name change.

7. If required, appear for the Court hearing.

Initial Filing

Original documents with original signatures (and Notary seals) should be filed. Copies of the documents may also be required by the Court. Retain a copy of any document which you sign or file for your own records. This filing is usually made in-person, at the District Court Clerk's Office. Documents to be included in the initial filing:

Petition for Change of Name of Minor (signed by one or both parents, or managing conservators, guardians or other persons given legal rights to the child in a court order), and a copy of the child's birth certificate

Minor's Consent to Change Name (signed by the minor if he/she is at least 10 years old)

Affidavit of Self-Representation

Agreed Order Changing Name of Minor

Texas Civil Case Information Sheet

Two self-addressed, stamped standard letter envelopes.

NOTE: The filing fee must be paid during your initial filing. Bring the payment.

NOTE: Depending on local circumstances and local Court procedures, the Order Setting and Hearing document may be needed as part of your initial filing, may be needed later, or may not be needed at all. Please work with your local Court Clerk to determine if a hearing will be needed, whether this Order document (or a variation of it) will be needed, and when it should be filed.

The Clerk will file your original documents and should stamp your copy(ies) and then give them back to you. These stamped copies are hereafter called "file-stamped" copies. As stated earlier, the Clerk will assign your case a "Cause Number" and a "Judicial District".

Make note of these assignments (your Cause Number and your Judicial District) because when you file your signed Order document as part of this same name change action, you will need to insert the Cause Number and Judicial District assigned by the Court in your document.

Once you file your Petition and Civil Case Information Sheet, if applicable, ask the Clerk how to schedule a meeting with a Judge for your child's name change documents to be reviewed by the Court.

Day of the Hearing

In some cases, no Court appearance or oral testimony before a Judge will be required. However, be aware that Court hearings for name change may be required, depending on your local jurisdiction, and almost always if there is an objection. The determining factor in whether a hearing will be required may be from the contents of the papers submitted to the Court Clerk. If there are objections to your Petition, the Court may require a hearing. Otherwise, the Clerk may take the liberty to pass the Petition to the Judge and recommend that the Petition be approved.

If a hearing is required, make sure that you (and all Petitioners in the Petition) arrive at the Courthouse for the hearing at least fifteen to thirty minutes early to avoid any complications. Take with you all paperwork not yet submitted and copies of what has already been submitted. Get your file from the District Court Clerk's office. Remember: Your Order should be filled out except for the Judge's signature. Typically, upon checking in, the Clerk/bailiff will direct you to the courtroom.

The hearing will be informal, may be recorded by a Court reporter, and, as long as there are no objections (see applicable section), it should not last over ten minutes. The Judge may require the child to come forward and testify.

Answer the Judge's questions with respect for the Court. Do not interrupt the Judge or volunteer information and always call the Judge "Your Honor." Expect the Judge's line of questioning to be somewhat similar to:

Do you truthfully swear that the statements in the Petition are true and accurate?

What is your name and address?

What is your relation to the child?

What is the child's name?

What is the child's address (in Texas)?

How old is the child?

What is the new name you are seeking for the child?

Is the name change being done for a fraudulent purpose?

What is the reason for wanting to change the child's name?

Is the father (or mother) joining in this Petition or otherwise consenting to the name change? (If no, why not?)

Is the child subject to continuing jurisdiction?

Is the child required to register as a sex offender?

Will the name change be in the best interests of the child?

If the Court is satisfied that the required information has been provided in the Petition, that the change of name is in the interest or to the benefit of the minor child and in the public interest, and if there are no reasonable objections to the name change, the Court may grant the Order (complete and sign the Order Granting Change of Name of a Minor) authorizing the change of name.

File the signed Order and return your file at the District Court Clerk's office.

Request your Change of Name Certificate (from the Court).

Objections to Your Request

If anyone files an objection to your request, your case will become a contested case and you are strongly urged to hire an attorney. If you retain no attorney you will have to represent yourself in a contested hearing.

Implementing the Change of Name

After the change of name has been finalized (ordered/decreed) you should notify several agencies.

• The Social Security Administration - fill out the "Request for Change in Social Security Records" form at your local Social Security Office. You will also need identification with the child's former name and a certified copy of the Court order changing his/her name; More information is available at 1-800-772-1213 or online at http://ssa-custhelp.ssa.gov/app/answers/detail/a_id/315/;

• Motor Vehicle Administration (driver's license and car registration) – if applicable, take a certified copy of the Court Order to the State Department of Motor Vehicles (Department of Public Safety – www.txdps.state.tx.us);

• Birth Certificates – Texas Bureau of Vital Statistics. (888-963-7111 and/or http://www.dshs.state.tx.us/VS/);

• Doctor offices, school records, sports organizations, welfare or child support payments, the United States Postal Service, Passport Office, etc.

• You may also wish to contact other places as well such as your bank if the minor's name is on any accounts. Should you need extra copies of the Order they should be available from the Clerk's office at a nominal fee.

IMPORTANT NOTE: After changing one's name, it is always a good idea to revise any legal document(s) that is/are in force that may include the name of the child.

Forms for two Petitioners (Joint Petitioners)

CAUSE NO._____

IN RE:	§ § § §	IN THE _____ JUDICIAL DISTRICT OF
CHANGE OF NAME OF	§ §	
_____	§ §	_____ COUNTY, TEXAS
A MINOR	§ § §	NO. _____

ORIGINAL PETITION FOR CHANGE OF NAME OF MINOR

TO THE HONORABLE COURT:

_____ and _____,
Petitioners, bring this suit requesting that the name of _____, a
minor, be changed to _____ and show:

1. Petitioner, _____, is the [ ] parent [ ] managing
conservator [ ] legal guardian of the minor.

The second Petitioner, _____, is the [ ] parent
[ ] managing conservator [ ] legal guardian of the minor.

2. _____, a minor [ ] male [ ] female, was born on
_____ in the city and state of _____.

A copy of the birth certificate is attached to this Petition.

His/Her social security number is: _____.

[ ] His/Her driver's license number is _____ issued in the State of
_____.

[ ] He/She does not have a driver's license.

3. _____ is _____ years old, and resides at
_____, in the city of
_____, _____ County, Texas.

4. _____ is not subject to continuing jurisdiction of any court
under Chapter 155 of the Texas Family Code.

or

_____ is subject to continuing jurisdiction of a court under Chapter 155 of the Texas Family Code.

The type of case is _____, Case Number _____, type of Court _____, County and State of Court _____.

5. _____ is not required to register as a sex offender, under Chapter 62 of the Texas Code of Criminal Procedure.

6. Petitioners request that the name of _____ be changed to _____.

7. Petitioners request the name change for the following reasons:

_____
_____
_____
_____
_____.

WHEREFORE, Petitioners request that the Court order that the name of the minor, _____, be changed to _____.

Petitioners swear under oath that the facts stated in this petition are true and correct.

(This document should only be signed in the presence of a Notary Public.)

_____   _____
Date   Petitioner,_____
                      _____
                      _____

State of Texas
County of   _____

Sworn to and subscribed before me, the undersigned authority, on _____ (date) by _____.

(Notary seal)   _____
                       (Notary's signature)

_____   _____
Date   Petitioner,_____

                           _____

                           _____

State of Texas
County of   _____

Sworn to and subscribed before me, the undersigned authority, on _____ (date) by

_____.

(Notary seal)   _____

                           (Notary's signature)

CAUSE NO._____

IN RE:	§	IN THE _____
	§	JUDICIAL DISTRICT OF
	§	
	§	
CHANGE OF NAME OF	§	
	§	
_____	§	_____ COUNTY, TEXAS
	§	
	§	
A MINOR	§	NO. _____

CHILD'S CONSENT TO CHANGE NAME

I, _____, consent to the legal change of my name from _____ to _____.

I am _____ years old.

The name change is for me.

_____
Printed name of Minor (child to print his/her name)

_____
Date

_____
SIGNATURE OF MINOR

STATE OF TEXAS
COUNTY OF _____

Sworn to and subscribed before me, the undersigned authority, on _____ (date) by _____.

Notary Public, State of Texas

_____
Print/Type Name
Commission Expires: _____

CAUSE NO._____

IN RE: § IN THE _____
§ JUDICIAL DISTRICT OF
§
§
CHANGE OF NAME OF §
§
§
_____ § _____ COUNTY, TEXAS
§
§
A MINOR § NO. _____

AFFIDAVIT OF SELF-REPRESENTATION

_____, being first duly sworn, deposes and says:

That she is the [ ] parent [ ] managing conservator [ ] legal guardian of _____, and that she is seeking this Change of Name of a Minor on behalf of _____, a minor, without the assistance of legal counsel.

_____   _____

Date   Petitioner - _____

State of Texas
County of   _____

Sworn to and subscribed before me, the undersigned authority, on _____ (date) by _____.

(Notary seal)   _____
                       (Notary's signature)

_____, being first duly sworn, deposes and says:

That he is the [ ] parent [ ] managing conservator [ ] legal guardian of _____, and that he is seeking this Change of Name of a Minor on behalf of _____, a minor, without the assistance of legal counsel.

_____   _____

Date   Petitioner - _____

State of Texas

County of _____

Sworn to and subscribed before me, the undersigned authority, on _____ (date) by
_____.

(Notary seal)   _____

                                 (Notary's signature)

CAUSE NO._____

IN RE:	§	**IN THE** _____
	§	**JUDICIAL DISTRICT OF**
	§	
	§	
CHANGE OF NAME OF	§	
	§	
_____	§	_____ **COUNTY, TEXAS**
	§	
	§	
A MINOR	§	**NO.** _____

<u>AGREED ORDER CHANGING NAME OF MINOR</u>

On _____, this Court heard the Original Petition for Change of Name of Minor of _____, a minor.

Petitioners _____ and _____
Appeared in person, presented the Petition, and announced ready.

The Court finds that it has jurisdiction of the case and of the minor.

___ Testimony was not recorded. -- or --
___ Testimony was recorded by the official court reporter of the Court.

The Court finds the following information about the minor:

1. _____, a minor [ ] male [ ] female, was born on _____ in the city and state of _____.

2. _____ is _____ years old, and resides at _____, in the city of _____, _____ County, Texas.

3. _____ is not subject to continuing jurisdiction of any court under Chapter 155 of the Texas Family Code.

or

_____ is subject to continuing jurisdiction of a court under Chapter 155 of the Texas Family Code.

The type of case is _____, Case Number _____, type of Court _____, County and State of Court _____.

4. _____ has a Social Security Number of
_____.

[ ] His/Her driver's license number is _____ issued in the State of
_____.

[ ] He/She does not have a driver's license.

After considering the pleadings, evidence, and arguments of the parties, the Court finds that the change of name requested in the Petition is in the best interests of _____ and is in the interest of the public.

IT IS, THEREFORE, ORDERED that the name of _____ is changed to _____.

IT IS FURTHER ORDERED that a copy of this order be sent to the Texas Bureau of Vital Statistics pursuant to Family Code Section 45.004.

SIGNED THIS _____ DAY OF _____, 20 _____.

_____
JUDGE PRESIDING

CAUSE NO._____

IN RE:	§	IN THE _____
	§	JUDICIAL DISTRICT OF
	§	
	§	
CHANGE OF NAME OF	§	
	§	
_____	§	_____ COUNTY, TEXAS
	§	
	§	
A MINOR	§	NO. _____

ORDER SETTING AND HEARING FORM

Pursuant to the procedures of the Court, the above-entitled and numbered Petition for Change of Name shall be set for a non-jury hearing at the following date, time, duration and location:

_____

_____

_____

_____

All Petitioners shall be provided appropriate prior notice of this hearing, and shall be entitled to appear before this Court to give testimony or bear witness to this action.

SIGNED THIS _____ DAY OF _____, 20 _____.

_____
JUDGE PRESIDING

CIVIL CASE INFORMATION SHEET

Cause Number (For Clerk Use Only): _____ Court (For Clerk Use Only):

_____

Styled: <u>IN RE: Change of Name of</u> _____, a minor

A civil case information sheet must be completed and submitted when an original petition or application is filed to initiate a new civil, family law, probate, or mental health case or when a post-judgment petition for modification or motion for enforcement is filed in a family law case. The information should be the best available at the time of filing. This sheet, approved by the Texas Judicial Council, is intended to collect information that will be used for statistical purposes only. It neither replaces nor supplements the filings or service of pleading or other documents as required by law or rule. The sheet does not constitute a discovery request, response, or supplementation, and it is not admissible at trial.

1. Contact information for person completing case information sheet:

Name:

_____

Address:

_____
_____

E-mail.

_____

Telephone:

_____

Fax:

_____

State Bar No:
N/A

Signature:

_____

Names of parties in case:

Plaintiff(s)/Petitioner(s):

_____
_____

Defendant(s)/Respondent(s):
N/A

Person or entity completing sheet is:
[ ]   Attorney for Plaintiff/Petitioner
[X]   Pro Se Plaintiff/Petitioner
[ ]   Title IV-D Agency
[ ]   Other: _____

2. Indicate case type, or identify the most important issue in the case:

Family Law

Other Family Law
        [ ]   Enforce Foreign Judgment
        [ ]   Habeas Corpus

[X]   Name Change
[ ]   Protective Order
[ ]   Removal of Disabilities of Minority
[ ]   Other: _____

Forms for Individual Petitioner (sole Petitioner)

CAUSE NO._____

IN RE:	§ § § §	IN THE _____ JUDICIAL DISTRICT OF
CHANGE OF NAME OF	§ §	
_____	§ §	_____ COUNTY, TEXAS
A MINOR	§ § §	NO. _____

ORIGINAL PETITION FOR CHANGE OF NAME OF MINOR

TO THE HONORABLE COURT:

_____, Petitioner, brings this suit requesting that the name of _____, a minor, be changed to _____ and shows:

1. Petitioner, _____, is the [ ] parent [ ] managing conservator [ ] legal guardian of the minor.

There is no Co-Petitioner because:

[ ] the parental rights of the other parent have been terminated. (A court order of termination is attached.)

[ ] the other parent of the minor is deceased. (A copy of the death certificate is attached.)

2. _____, a minor [ ] male [ ] female, was born on _____ in the city and state of _____.

A copy of the birth certificate is attached to this Petition.

His/her social security number is: _____.

[ ] His/her driver's license number is _____ issued in the State of _____.

[ ] He/she does not have a driver's license.

3. _____ is _____ years old, and resides at _____, in the city of _____, _____ County, Texas.

4. _____ is not subject to continuing jurisdiction of any court under Chapter 155 of the Texas Family Code.

or

_____ is subject to continuing jurisdiction of a court under Chapter 155 of the Texas Family Code.

The type of case is _____, Case Number _____, type of Court _____, County and State of Court _____.

5. _____ is not required to register as a sex offender, under Chapter 62 of the Texas Code of Criminal Procedure.

6. Petitioner requests that the name of _____ be changed to _____.

7. Petitioner requests the name change for the following reasons:

_____

_____

_____

_____

_____.

WHEREFORE, Petitioner requests that the Court order that the name of the minor, _____, be changed to _____.

Petitioner swears under oath that the facts stated in this petition are true and correct.

(This document should only be signed in the presence of a Notary Public.)

_____   _____
Date   Petitioner,_____
                        _____
                        _____

State of Texas
County of _____

Sworn to and subscribed before me, the undersigned authority, on _____ (date) by _____.

(Notary seal)   _____
                       (Notary's signature)

CAUSE NO._____

IN RE:	§	IN THE _____
	§	JUDICIAL DISTRICT OF
	§	
	§	
	§	
CHANGE OF NAME OF	§	
	§	
_____	§	_____ COUNTY, TEXAS
	§	
	§	
A MINOR	§	NO. _____

CHILD'S CONSENT TO CHANGE NAME

I, _____, consent to the legal change of my name from _____ to _____.

I am _____ years old.

The name change is for me.

_____
Printed name of minor (child to print his/her name)

_____
Date

_____
SIGNATURE OF MINOR

STATE OF TEXAS
COUNTY OF _____

Sworn to and subscribed before me, the undersigned authority, on _____ (date) by _____.

Notary Public, State of Texas

_____
Print/Type Name
Commission Expires: _____

CAUSE NO._____

IN RE: §   IN THE _____
                                         §   JUDICIAL DISTRICT OF
                                         §
                                         §
CHANGE OF NAME OF   §
                                         §
_____   §   _____ COUNTY, TEXAS
                                         §
                                         §
A MINOR   §   NO. _____

AFFIDAVIT OF SELF-REPRESENTATION

_____, being first duly sworn, deposes and says:

That he/she is the [ ] parent [ ] managing conservator [ ] legal guardian of _____, and that he/she is seeking this Change of Name of a Minor on behalf of _____, a minor, without the assistance of legal counsel.

_____   _____
Date   Petitioner,_____

State of Texas
County of   _____

Sworn to and subscribed before me, the undersigned authority, on _____ (date) by
_____.

(Notary seal)   _____
                           (Notary's signature)

CAUSE NO._____

IN RE: §   IN THE _____
                                §   JUDICIAL DISTRICT OF
                                §
                                §
                                §
CHANGE OF NAME OF   §
                                §
_____ §   _____ COUNTY, TEXAS
                                §
                                §
A MINOR   §   NO. _____

AGREED ORDER CHANGING NAME OF MINOR

On _____, this Court heard the Original Petition for Change of Name of Minor of _____, a minor.

Petitioner, _____, appeared in person, presented the Petition, and announced ready.

There is no Co-Petitioner because

[ ] the child's other parent has no parental rights as terminated by court order

[ ] the child's other parent is deceased.

The Court finds that it has jurisdiction of the case and of the minor.

____ Testimony was not recorded. -- or --
____ Testimony was recorded by the official court reporter of the Court.

The Court finds the following information about the minor:

1. _____, a minor [ ] male [ ] female, was born on _____ in the city and state of _____.

2. _____ is _____ years old, and resides at _____, in the city of _____, _____ County, Texas.

3. _____ is not subject to continuing jurisdiction of any court under Chapter 155 of the Texas Family Code.

or

_____ is subject to continuing jurisdiction of a court under Chapter 155 of the Texas Family Code.

The type of case is _____, Case Number _____, type of Court _____, County and State of Court _____.

4. _____ has a Social Security Number of _____.

[ ] His/her driver's license number is _____ issued in the State of _____.

[ ] He/she does not have a driver's license.

After considering the pleadings, evidence, and arguments of the parties, the Court finds that the change of name requested in the Petition is in the best interests of _____ and is in the interest of the public.

IT IS, THEREFORE, ORDERED that the name of _____ is changed to _____.

IT IS FURTHER ORDERED that a copy of this order be sent to the Texas Bureau of Vital Statistics pursuant to Family Code Section 45.004.

SIGNED THIS _____ DAY OF _____, 20 _____.

_____
JUDGE PRESIDING

CAUSE NO._____

IN RE: §   IN THE _____
       §   JUDICIAL DISTRICT OF
       §
       §
CHANGE OF NAME OF §
       §
       §
_____ §   _____ COUNTY, TEXAS
       §
       §
A MINOR §   NO. _____

ORDER SETTING AND HEARING FORM

Pursuant to the procedures of the Court, the above-entitled and numbered Petition for Change of Name shall be set for a non-jury hearing at the following date, time, duration and location:

_____

_____

_____

_____

All Petitioners shall be provided appropriate prior notice of this hearing, and shall be entitled to appear before this Court to give testimony or bear witness to this action.

SIGNED THIS _____ DAY OF _____, 20 _____.

_____
JUDGE PRESIDING

CIVIL CASE INFORMATION SHEET

Cause Number (For Clerk Use Only): _____   Court (For Clerk Use Only):
_____

Styled: <u>IN RE: Change of Name of</u> _____, a minor

A civil case information sheet must be completed and submitted when an original petition or application is filed to initiate a new civil, family law, probate, or mental health case or when a post-judgment petition for modification or motion for enforcement is filed in a family law case. The information should be the best available at the time of filing. This sheet, approved by the Texas Judicial Council, is intended to collect information that will be used for statistical purposes only. It neither replaces nor supplements the filings or service of pleading or other documents as required by law or rule. The sheet does not constitute a discovery request, response, or supplementation, and it is not admissible at trial.

1. Contact information for person completing case information sheet:

Name:

_____

Address:

_____
_____

E-mail.

_____

Telephone:

_____

Fax:

_____

State Bar No:
N/A

Signature:

_____

Names of parties in case:

Plaintiff(s)/Petitioner(s):

_____

Defendant(s)/Respondent(s):
N/A

Person or entity completing sheet is:
[ ]   Attorney for Plaintiff/Petitioner
[X]   Pro Se Plaintiff/Petitioner
[ ]   Title IV-D Agency
[ ]   Other: _____

2. Indicate case type, or identify the most important issue in the case:

Family Law

Other Family Law
    [ ]   Enforce Foreign Judgment
    [ ]   Habeas Corpus

[**X**]   Name Change
[ ]   Protective Order
[ ]   Removal of Disabilities of Minority
[ ]   Other: _____

Need Legal Advice from a Virtual Attorney?

There is a new breed of lawyer that is committed to providing fixed fee limited legal services over the Internet. Often called "virtual lawyers" these practitioners offer legal advice for a fixed fee online and many offer name change legal forms bundled with legal advice also for a fixed fee.

- Lawyers who offer their legal services online offer these benefits:
- Lower overhead means lower fees;
- Fast Service;
- Accessible 24 x 7;
- Convenience – you don't have to give up hours during your work day to meet with a lawyer face to face in a downtown office building.

Check out SmartLegalForm's nationwide Directory of Virtual Law Firms at http://www.directlawconnect.com.

⟡ DirectLaw

Do You Want Your Documents Reviewed by a Legal Document Assistant?

SmartLegalForms employs a team of legal document assistants, also known as Legal Technicians, who will provide a review of your forms to make sure that you have answered every question and that spelling and other information is internally consistent. We cannot give you legal advice. This service is available at the Web site: http://www.texasnamechangelaw.com. When you take advantage of this service we give you a credit for the price you paid for this book towards the Legal Document Preparation Service Fee.

For additional information, just email: support@smartlegalforms.com indicating the date of purchase of this book in the subject line of your email. You can also call our Help Line at: 1-800-481-1025